ALWAYS
A FRIEND

Written and Compiled by
Ellyn Sanna

BARBOUR
PUBLISHING, INC.

1

Life's Best Treasure

Ointment and perfume rejoice the heart:
so doth the sweetness of
a man's friend by hearty counsel. . . .
Iron sharpeneth iron;
so a man sharpeneth the
countenance of his friend.

PROVERBS 27:9, 17

Presented to

_____

On the occasion of

_____

From

_____

Date

_____

Published by Barbour Publishing, Inc., P.O. Box 719, Uhrichsville, Ohio 44683
http://www.barbourbooks.com

Member of the
Evangelical Christian
Publishers Association

Printed in China.

*I*magine what life would be like without your friends. No one to call when you have a fight with your husband. No one with whom to share coffee and laughter. No one to cry with you when everything is going wrong, no one to be glad for you when everything is going right. No one with whom to share your thoughts, no one to pray for you.

Thank God for your friends. We can get by without money and prestige and new possessions—but the thought of getting by without our friends is too painful to imagine. They are truly one of life's greatest treasures.

*The best that we find in our travels is
an honest friend.
He is a fortunate voyager who finds
many.*

ROBERT LOUIS STEVENSON

Dear God, thank You for my friends. Help me not to take them for granted. Sometimes my priorities get twisted up so easily; I start thinking that money and possessions are more important than people. Your Son's life shows me that You treasure individuals far more than You care about earthly prestige or power or wealth. Remind me often how poor my life would be without the friends You've given me. Help me to enrich their lives as they have mine. Amen.

*Of our mixed life
two quests are given control:
food for the body,
friendship for the soul.*

ARTHUR UPSON

$\mathcal{W}$e are the weakest of spendthrifts if we let one friend drop off through inattention, or let one push away another, or if we hold aloof from one for petty jealousy or heedless roughness. Would you throw away a diamond because it pricked you? One good friend is not to be weighed against all the jewels of the earth.

WILL CARLETON

*True happiness
consists not in
the multitude of friends,
but in their worth and choice.*

BEN JONSON

2

The Gift of
a Friend's Love

"This is my command:
Love each other."

JOHN 15:17 NIV

Friendship is an education. It draws the friend out of himself and all that is selfish and ignoble in him and leads him to life's higher levels of altruism and sacrifice. Many a man has been saved from a life of frivolity and emptiness to a career of noble service by finding at a critical hour the right kind of friend.

G. D. Prentice

If a friend is in trouble, don't annoy him by asking if there is anything you can do. Think up something appropriate and do it.

Edgar Watson Howe

Love is a choice—
not simply or necessarily a rational choice,
but rather a willingness to be
present to others without pretense or guile.

CARTER HEYWARD

Among those whom I like,
I can find no common denominator,
but among those whom I love, I can:
All of them make me laugh.

W. H. AUDEN

*H*appy is the house that shelters a friend! . . . I awoke this morning with devout thanksgiving for my friends, the old and the new. . . . High thanks I owe you, excellent lovers, who carry out the world for me to new and noble depths, and enlarge the meaning of all my thoughts. . . .

There are two elements that go to the composition of friendship, each so sovereign that I can detect no superiority in either, no reason why either should be first named. One is truth. A friend is a person with whom I can be sincere. Before him I may think aloud. I. . .may deal with him with the simplicity and wholeness with which one atom meets another. . . .

The other element of friendship is tenderness. . . . The only way to have a friend is to be one.

RALPH WALDO EMERSON

$\mathcal{I}$ don't meddle with what
my friends believe or reject,
any more than I ask whether
they are rich or poor; I love them.

JAMES RUSSELL LOWELL

A brother may not be a friend,
but a friend will always be a brother.

BENJAMIN FRANKLIN

$\mathcal{I}$ never considered
a difference of opinion in politics,
in religion, in philosophy,
as cause for withdrawing from a friend.

THOMAS JEFFERSON

3

Hearts that Understand

Out of the abundance of the heart
the mouth speaketh.

MATTHEW 12:34

A friend is a person
with whom you dare to be yourself.

FRANK CRANE

A true test of friendship—
to sit or walk with a friend for an hour in
perfect silence without wearying of one another's company.

DINAH MULOCK CRAIK

The language of friendship
is not words,
but meanings.
It is an intelligence above language.

HENRY DAVID THOREAU

Dear God, thank You for understanding friends. Thank You that so often we're on the same wavelength, laughing together, crying together, encouraging each other with our understanding. I'm grateful that I'm not alone, that I can share my life with my friends. And when I listen to them, give me a heart that understands. Amen.

Friendship. . .
is an Union of Spirits,
a Marriage of Hearts.

WILLIAM PENN

$\mathcal{B}$ut, after all, the very best thing in good talk, and the thing that helps most, is friendship. How it dissolves the barriers that divide us, and loosens all constraint, and diffuses itself like some fine old cordial through all the veins of life—this feeling that we understand and trust each other, and wish each other heartily well! Everything into which it really comes is good.

HENRY VAN DYKE

One of the most beautiful qualities of true friendship is to understand and to be understood.

SENECA

If therefore there is any encouragement in Christ, if there is any consolation of love, if there is any fellowship of the Spirit, if any affection and compassion, make my joy complete by being of the same mind, maintaining the same love, united in spirit, intent on one purpose.

PHILIPPIANS 2:1–2 NAS

Being with people you like and respect is so meaningful. Perhaps you have known some of them most of your life. Having friends around for a pleasant evening is one of life's most cherished joys as far as I am concerned. But when those with me are fellow believers how much greater that joy is, for we know that it will be rekindled, one day, in eternity.

JAMES STEWART

4

Sharing Joy, Sharing Sorrow

So encourage each other to
build each other up,
just as you are already doing.

1 Thessalonians 5:11 TLB

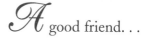Friendship renders prosperity more brilliant,
while it lightens adversity by sharing it
and making its burden common.

CICERO

A good friend...

- makes a hot fudge sundae taste even better.
- calms us down when we're angry.
- shares our tears.
- laughs at the same things we do.
- prays for us when we're too weak to
  pray for ourselves.

"Unbosom yourself," said Wimsey.
"Trouble shared is trouble halved."

DOROTHY SAYERS

$\mathcal{T}$wo are better than one. . . .
If one falls down, his friend can help him up.
But pity the man who falls and
has no one to help him up!

ECCLESIASTES 4:9–10 NIV

To have joy one must share it—
happiness was born a twin.

LORD BYRON

Dear God, I am grateful for the friends who participate in both my joys and sorrows. My discouragement is never so overwhelming when my friends help me carry it, and I find meaning even in my life's greatest sorrows. Laughter shared is twice as hilarious, and I take the deepest satisfaction in my life's blessing when I share them with my friends. Thank You for giving us the ability to communicate our feelings to each other; thank You for sending Your Spirit to us through our friends. Amen.

*Carry each other's burdens,
and in this way you will
fulfill the law of Christ.*

GALATIANS 6:2 NIV

5

A Friend's Forgiveness

Be kind and compassionate to one another,
forgiving each other,
just as in Christ God forgave you.

EPHESIANS 4:32 NIV

A true friend forgives you even when. . .

- you forget her birthday.
- you act like a brat when she forgets your birthday.
- you stand her up for a lunch date two times in a row.
- you borrow her favorite jacket and spill tomato sauce on it.
- you can't stop talking about the fight you had with your mother, even though you know she wants to talk about her new job.

He who throws away a friend is as bad as he who throws away his life.

SOPHOCLES

Dear God, help me to forgive my friends when they seem to let me down. Remind me that only You are perfect; only You can always be there and always understand me. Thank You for all the times my friends forgive me. I never seem to use up their forgiveness; thank You for showing Your own nature through them. Amen.

Two persons cannot long be friends if they cannot forgive each other's little failings.

JEAN DE LA BRUYÈRE

*T*hen came Peter to him, and said,
Lord, how oft shall my brother sin against me,
and I forgive him? till seven times?
Jesus saith unto him, I say not unto thee,
Until seven times: but, Until seventy times seven.

MATTHEW 18:21–22

*W*e can have no relationship of depth or authenticity
if we insist there is nothing wrong with us, or
that it is always the other person's fault. . . . To
refuse to take responsibility and admit our
flaws makes the intimacy and love we seek in
relationships an impossibility.

REBECCA MANLEY PIPPERT

$\mathcal{D}$o not be sensitive. Perhaps you are by nature, but you can get over it with the exercise of common sense and the help of God. Let things hurt until the tender spot gets callous. . . . Sensitiveness is only another kind of self-consciousness, and as such we should seek deliverance from its irritating power.

ISABELLA THOBURN

Every man should have a fair-sized cemetery in which to bury the faults of his friends.

HENRY WARD BEECHER

$\mathcal{M}$y friend is not perfect—
nor am I—
and so we suit each other admirably.

ALEXANDER POPE

6

Old Friends

I thank my God
every time I remember you.

PHILIPPIANS 1:3 NIV

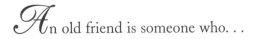

*A*n old friend is someone who. . .

- remembers what you looked like in seventh grade.
- knows the name of the first boy you loved.
- doesn't tell your children all the rules you broke
  when you were a teenager.
- knows a few things about you that even your
  husband doesn't know.
- has known you through all the changes in your life—
  and still loves you.

As gold more splendid
from the fire appears,
thus friendship brightens
by the length of years.

THOMAS CARLYLE

Dear God, thank You for my old friends. I'm grateful for their faithful friendship. Thank You for the comfort they give me when the world seems overwhelming. Thank You for the laughter they've brought into my life over the years. I'm glad our friendship will last into eternity. Amen.

There is no better looking-glass than an old friend.

THOMAS FULLER

7

New Friends

I was a stranger,
and ye took me in.

MATTHEW 25:35

$\mathscr{Y}$ou know you've made a new friend when. . .

- you find yourselves laughing at the same jokes.
- you discover you like the same books and movies.
- you find yourselves talking faster and faster, trying to find out everything about each other.
- you realize you share the same faith in God.
- the differences you find only make the other person seem more interesting.

$\mathscr{W}$e do not make friends
as we make houses,
but discover them as we do the arbutus,
under the leaves of our lives,
concealed in our experience.

WILLIAM RADER

$\mathcal{B}$lessed are they who have the gift of making friends,
for it is one of God's best gifts.
It involves many things,
but above all the power of going out of one's self,
and appreciating what is noble and loving in another.

THOMAS HUGHES

*How can we tell what coming people are
aboard the ships that may be sailing
to us now from the unknown seas?*

CHARLES DICKENS

*$\mathcal{D}$ear God, thank You for the new friends You
send into my life. Help me never to think I have all
the friends I need. Remind me that You have new
ways to touch me through each person that I meet.
Amen.*

8

Even Across the Miles

May the LORD keep watch
between you and me when
we are away from each other.

GENESIS 31:49 NIV

*N*othing makes the earth seem so spacious
as to have friends at a distance:
They make the latitudes and longitudes.

HENRY DAVID THOREAU

*E*ven across the miles,
true friends stay in touch with each other by. . .

- talking on the phone.
- writing letters.
- sending E-mail.
- remembering.
- praying.

*What joy is better than
the news of friends?*

ROBERT BROWNING

*As cold waters
to a thirsty soul,
so is good news
from a far country.*

PROVERBS 25:25

Dear God, be with my friends even when we can't be together. Thank You that miles have no meaning in eternity. Amen.

9

A Glimpse of God

No one has ever seen God;
but if we love one another,
God lives in us and his love is
made complete in us.

1 JOHN 4:12 NIV

Every true friend is a glimpse of God.

LUCY LARCOM

*O*ur friends are like God when they. . .

- stick by us through all the changes in our lives.
- forgive us over and over.
- never stop listening and caring and understanding.
- give themselves to us.
- love us no matter what.

*T*he more we love, the better we are;
and the greater our friendships are,
the dearer we are to God.

JEREMY TAYLOR

*H*uman love and the delights of friendship,
out of which are built the memories that endure,
are also to be treasured up as hints
of what shall be hereafter.

BEDE JARRETT

*W*e need not set out in search for a friend. . .
rather, we must simply set out to be
the friend Christ modeled—
anticipating the needs of others,
wearing ourselves out at giving.
Jesus died doing it.

JOY MACKENZIE

*H*oly Friendship that has medicine for
all the wretchedness is not to be despised.
From God it truly is,
that amid the wretchedness of this exile,
we be comforted with the counsel of friends
until we come to Him.

RICHARD ROLLE

*D*ear God, thank You for all my faithful
friends. Their understanding, their forgiveness,
their love all help me comprehend Your love a little more. Thank You for showing me Yourself
through them. May they see You in me. Amen.

$\mathcal{G}$od is the best Friend because. . .

- He always understands.
- He's never too busy to listen.
- we can never be separated from His love.
- He knows us better than we know ourselves.
- He loves us more than anyone else ever could.